GUIDE TO A WINNING INTERVIEW

Questions and Answers for Job Interview Success. How to Be More Confident, Be Yourself and Answer Interview Questions.

Jim Hunting

Table of Contents

Introduction

Whether you are a fresh college graduate or someone who is looking to kick start a new career, one of the things that you should be fully cognizant of is the dynamics of the job-hunting process including of course the often-dreaded interview portion.

While there is no right way to do an interview, there are a couple of pointers that you should take note and be mindful of to make sure that your interview goes well and hopefully helps you land your target job.

However, even before embarking on a job-hunting adventure, it is essential that you develop a deep sense of self-awareness. Knowing who you are, what your values and competencies are, as well as what your goals are will help you in coming up with a clearer vision of your future self.

Know what you do best.

Applying for a job should always be preceded by identifying the things that you are capable of doing well. A longstanding problem in the labor market is the apparent mismatch of jobs available and the skill set of the labor pool. If you want to have a job that you are competent and fully comfortable in, you should look for positions that cater to your abilities and strengths.

Find your market.

If you are looking for a job in the finance industry, it makes sense that you look for one in a financial district. If you are looking for an arts-related profession, you need to factor in the available art venues and spaces in a particular place. On some occasions, this might mean that you have to step out of your comfort zone and move in to an entirely new area.

Know how much you are worth.

Since applying for a job is essentially a way of showcasing your knowledge and experience in a particular field, then it goes without saying that you should have a clear idea of how much you should be worth. Don't be afraid to aim for the best.

Improve on your skills, if you must.

Some jobs require specialized skills, experience or educational attainment. If you are keen on earning such kind of job, then you should take the time and effort to meet the basic criteria.

Have realistic and reasonable expectations.

Your excitement and enthusiasm over the prospect of getting a job you like should be guarded by reason and logic. This doesn't mean that you should sport a pessimistic outlook, either. Basically, you should have a way of gauging your abilities and your performance in the exercise of such abilities. You should be honest enough to admit if there's any weakness you should work on or conversely, highlight the strengths that you can use as leverage in the future.

Find the right motivation.

There is nothing more powerful than being motivated to reach your goals. But motivation comes in different forms for different people. Some see money as a powerful motivating factor. In choosing jobs, they go for openings with a relatively higher pay.

Meanwhile, other people lean more toward job opportunities that provide a profound sense of satisfaction and boost their sense of self-worth. When picking jobs, these people look at the culture of the workplace and gauge it based on how being part of this particular organization can make them better.

Ideal worker mindset

But no matter the motivation, an inarguably essential factor to take into account is the importance of developing an ideal worker mindset. You must come across as a perfect fit to the job opening that you are aiming for. Your skills, attitude and character must match the requirements of this particular employment opportunity.

A good way of making yourself better prepared for the challenges of job hunting is by making yourself familiar with the dynamics of the labor market, as well as the history and background of the specific organization that you want to be a part of including the working environment.

Chapter 1: Crafting Your Cover Letter

Now that you understand what a cover letter is and its importance, it is time to learn how to craft your own well-written letter, also known as a CV.

While there are many dos and don'ts in writing a cover letter, thankfully, there is a basic pattern that every professional cover letter should follow.

You can use this guideline with your own information to ensure that your CV is always the correct format.

A basic no-fuss cover letter should consist of:

- Your Name
- Phone number
- Email address
- Date
- Addressed to the name and professional title of the hiring manager
- Name of the company you are applying for a position at

This is the most basic of cover letter guidelines, as you can see, it doesn't even contain much information on the individual. This is because while the standard guideline above is needed, the rest of the letter can be highly personalized.

Along with the above guideline, you also must add other information. This can include a variety of components, depending upon the person. Some options include:

- The address of your professional website

- Your professional title

- Your home address

- Links to your LinkedIn or Twitter

- City of Residence

While you want to illustrate your personality in your cover letter, it is important to do so in a professional manner.

For instance, you want to use an email address that illustrates professionalism. Such as [your name]@gmail.com or email@[your website].com.

You never want to include unprofessional email addresses on your cover letter or resume, as this can be a deal breaker. If your email is something such as SexyTiger135@gmail.com   or

CottonCandyFTW@yahoo.com you will want to create a new email address for professional purposes.

Ideally, you want to stick with either Gmail or an email created with your own website domain, as these are seen as the most professional options.

Similarly, you should avoid using an email address that contains your current work information.

If your professional email address contains your current company or position, it is disrespectful to both your previous company and the new company to use this address.

Lastly, ensure that your contact information is consistent across the board. You want your resume, cover letter, and social media to all use the same information.

You now understand the basic format of your cover letter and the most important information to include in each and every CV. However, these are only the bare bones of a cover letter.

You still need to include information that will make the employer want to hire you. For that, follow the tips below to get a customized and successful letter.

Use the Proper Format

The cover letter, while it can show your personality, needs to remain professional.

For this reason, use the same formal format that you would for any professional or business matter.

For this, you want to use either Times New Roman, Calibri, or Arial fonts in size twelve or ten point.

When writing your name, contact information, and date align them along the top of the letter. Lastly, keep the cover letter to a single page with three or four short paragraphs.

Address the Hiring Manager

Some people may address this cover letter's to "whom it may concern," but this is bad practice.

This will make it appear that you either have not done enough research on the company or that you are mass producing this CV to send out to multiple companies.

Instead, you want to directly address your letter to the person who will be hiring you. This person's name may be written in the job posting.

However, if it is not, then try calling the main phone number for the company and asking for both the name and position of the hiring manager.

This may seem like an unnecessary step; however, it will leave a big impression on the hiring manager and increase your likelihood of getting hired.

This will also give you the opportunity to learn more about the company in general.

If you have any personal connections to the company and would-be colleges then feel free to subtly mention these connections.

By doing this, it gives the hiring manager the opportunity to ask the people who know you their opinion of your work ethic and capability.

Use Keywords

Often times, employers don't simply read through every cover letter they receive. Instead, they may run it through a filtering software that is meant to scan for keywords in resumes.

This software allows an employer to wade through resumes and cover letters, only reading those that match their preferred keywords of desired skills and experience.

In order to get your cover letter read, you need to naturally and conversationally incorporate key phrases and words that fit the job's description.

You can do this by mentioning how many years of experience you have, degree type, developed skills, communication and organization abilities, and any history you have in project management.

Some examples of keywords to use include:

- Skill Keywords:

- Planned, wrote, analyzed, designed, quantified, programmed, trained, taught, surveyed, organized, critiqued, inspected, assembled, solved, engineered, maintained, operated, administered, appraised, audited, budgeted, calculated, projected, researched, directed, developed, performed, acted, established, fashioned, illustrated, founded, programmed, coached, communicated, instructed, enabled, encouraged, guided, informed, built.

- Result-Oriented Keywords:

- Implemented, planned, managed, upgraded, assessed, strengthened, persuaded, initiated, adapted, oversaw, lead, redesigned, helped, launched, began, adopted, boosted, headed, operated, increased, trained, educated, reformulated, expanded, acquired, generated, produced, initiated.

- Self-Descriptive Keywords:

- Independent, creative, unique, attentive, dependable, responsible, ambitious, analytical, sensitive, reliable, enthusiastic, adaptable, logical, initiative, efficient, experienced, effective, sincere, productive, personable, instrumental, honest, adept, loyal, diplomatic, insightful.

Keep the First Paragraph Strong

At the beginning of your letter, you should start with a strong and personal greeting directly to the hiring manager.

But, don't slack off after this greeting.

It is vital to have a strong opening paragraph that catches their attention and draws them into reading your entire letter and your resume.

This means that you absolutely must avoid any misspellings or typos.

You also need to include something interesting about yourself that sets you apart from the crowd.

While the entire cover letter is important, the most important areas to strengthen are the beginning and then end.

After all, it is vital to make a good first impression and leave off with a good impression.

Highlight Relevant Details

In your cover letter, you are able to go into more detail on how and why you are a perfect fit for a job.

While a resume simply highlights your experience, the cover letter explains why this experience makes you an ideal fit.

Therefore, when highlighting your experiences, be sure to stick with experiences and reasoning that fits the specific job.

For instance, if you were a waiter and are now applying to a job in another field, it may not at first appear that it is a relevant experience. Yet, the cover letter allows you to explain why this experience actually makes you the best fit. You can take the time to explain that your interactions with customers, managing disputes, and working as a team will enable you to better do the new job, if you are hired. If possible, try to use data and numbers to explain your strengths, as employers like to see hard numbers.

Tie Yourself to the Company

Whenever possible, speak of yourself in relation to the company.

This will show the hiring manager that you have knowledge of the company and convey enthusiasm.

You can do this by mentioning how much you care about the company's vision or mission.

If you have followed the company or used their products/services of years, you can mention how much they have beneficially impacted your life.

Similarly, you want to speak within the letter as if you have already been hired.

For instance, imagine that you are speaking to a manager after being hired and they ask why you chose the company.

You can answer with your interest in the company and enthusiasm about working for them.

For instance: "When I discovered DreamCloud Animation was hiring, I simply knew I must apply. I had been searching for a company that truly makes a difference, where I could make an impact. I was inspired by the company and their mission to consistently produce high-quality animation that tells a story to warm people hearts and increase the appreciation of the seemingly mundane. I believe in the mission of DreamCloud Animation, and I wanted to work with you so that I too can make a difference."

Name the Position Title

It may seem simple, but it is important to add in the name of the job title you are applying for.

This helps the employer to know that you are knowledgeable and understand what you are applying for.

This can be done easily, as you can say something to the effect of "Regarding the Graphic Design position," *or* "I am writing to apply for Floor Manager position [company name] recently advertised."

Illustrate How You Can Solve a Specific Problem

Are you a problem-solver? While stating this in a cover letter may seem beneficial, it actually has little impact on the hiring manager.

After all, what problems can you solve? By simply stating you are a problem-solver you might as well be saying you know how to "solve" the problem of not knowing what to eat for breakfast when the pantry is nearly bare.

Instead of telling the hiring manager that you are great at solving problems, detail exactly what problems you can help them solve.

How can you use your skills to help the company better and solve their problems? Take time to consider exactly what you can do for the company and then detail it.

Share a Story

You want your cover letter to be captivating, interesting, and informative.

One of the most successful ways in which you can do this is by sharing a story or anecdote about yourself.

This can allow the employer to get a better idea of your personality, work style, and skills. Although, it is important to share the right story while keeping it short and sweet.

How do you know if a story is right for your cover letter?

You can start by looking at the job description and researching the company.

Once you understand the position and company well, you can compare your skills, talents, and experience compared to what they are looking for in an employee.

For instance, the company might be looking for a team player, someone with communication skills, and a person who is able to resolve conflicts, and a person who is able to train those under them.

Keeping these aspects in mind, you can consider your past and think of an anecdote that contains as many of these traits as possible.

For instance, you might have volunteered at a place in which you managed a team, kept everyone on good terms while resolving conflicts, trained newcomers, and communicated the needs of the day to those working with you.

You can share this anecdote, while specifically mentioning these skills and traits you made use of.

By being able to hear a story of how you specifically have used your skills and traits in the past a company can get a better idea of how you will work on the job.

Stay Honest

The worst mistake you can make in your cover letter is being dishonest.

Not only does this have moral implications, but it will also come back to bite you.

If you tell the company that you have an experience, talent, or skill that you don't actually have, then they will find out in the future.

They will soon learn that you are unable to do what you stated, and it will get you into trouble.

Instead, stay honest while putting your best foot forward and highlighting your actual skills and traits in the most positive light possible.

Be You, Stay Unique

The cover letter is created to set you apart from the crowd, which your resume alone is unable to do.

Yet, many people fail to capture any of their unique qualities into their CV, leaving the hiring manager unimpressed and on their way to the next candidate.

This all too often happens when a person uses phrases such as "Hello, I am John/Jane Smith. I am a hard-working, multi-tasking, and detail-oriented person. I was born to be a leader and believe I could help your company."

A hiring manager or employer isn't going to be interested in a basic cover letter template that sounds as if it could be created by anyone. Highlight how you are unique and stand out from the crowd.

You can do this by switching out common words. For instance, instead of saying you are a *"natural-born leader"* you might say *"I excel when leading a team."*

This helps your cover letter to sound different, catching a person's eye better.

However, the best way you can stay unique is to share your stories and personality.

Work these into the letter by sharing with the hiring manager stories and examples of how you can best help the company, excel in the position, and make use of your strengths.

Illustrate Your Goals, Passions, and Dreams

An employer doesn't only want to know your strengths and why you are qualified for a position, they also want to know why you care and the career path you envision.

After all, they know that the more passionate a person is about their work the more motivated they are to do a job well done.

If you are passionate about the career, express this. If you dream about becoming a manager and leading a team, let them know.

If your goal is to advance in your field, don't hesitate to add that.

An example: "Graphic design and integrating it into advertisements has been my passion for many years, which is why I pursued my degree in graphic design at New York University. Not only do I dream of working in this field, but I believe my skills will help me to excel. My enthusiasm, passion, and work ethic will push me forward to new heights, making me a wonderful candidate for the position of Graphic Designer at Think! Advertisements."

End on a High Note

When concluding your cover letter in the last paragraph, be sure to use one or two sentences to reiterate why you are the perfect candidate for the job.

As most people will read the resume directly after the cover letter, you want to use this final paragraph to highlight anything important that you want the manager to notice following in your resume.

After you have reiterated anything important, you want to mention that you have attached your resume and that you are looking forward to hearing back from them.

You might even give them a date by which you will contact them if you don't hear back.

For instance: "Thank you for taking the time to consider me for the position of Graphic Designer. I hope my resume, which I have included, proves to be helpful. I look forward to hearing back from you in the near future. I will stay in touch, making a phone call in one week, unless I hear back from you in the meantime."

Unique Visual Format

Humans naturally remember something when it stands out from the crowd. For this reason, instead of simply typing out and printing your cover letter, it is a good idea to give it a unique visual format.

However, this must be done carefully. You don't want to use bright and flashy gimmicks that will turn off the reader or make it more difficult to focus on the contents of the letter. This means that you want to avoid brightly colored paper, unusual fonts, more than two types of fonts, or colored fonts for the letter contents.

The cover letter must remain professional and easy to read.

If you do choose to play around with the visual format, look at some of our examples below to get an idea of what works.

While you want the body text of the letter to use black ink, you might decide to use a dark blue or green ink for the heading text.

Adding a picture of yourself doesn't hurt, as long as it doesn't take up too much of the page space.

Try to arrange your text on the page so that it is visually appealing, rather than appearing in one big difficult to read block.

While you shouldn't use brightly colored paper, you can use a high-quality white or off-white paper.

Chapter 2: Sell yourself like a pro

The job market today is more competitive than ever. Think of it this way:

It's easy to advertise a product when there are fewer competitors. All you need to do is to show the product to the consumer (example: show potential consumers an image of a bath soap and they'll buy it because they know what it's for.) However, if there are several similar products on the market, showing the consumers an image of the product is not enough to convince consumers to buy it. You have to remind them what it's for, how it will make their lives easier/better, and all the other reasons why they should buy it (this is when you start using commercial models, the perfect script, perfect background music, perfect packaging, etc.) More importantly, you have to show potential consumers why your product is better than all the others. It's for this reason why TV and printed ads strive to be more colorful, more interesting, and more unique.

And with the number of job-seekers out there, this is exactly how you should sell yourself as well.

What makes a great salesman great? It's when he's able to take control of the situation while making the clients believe that they're the ones in control. An experienced salesman will discuss the needs and concerns of the clients while persuading the customers that what he's selling is the answer to their problems.

A job interview is no different. View the interview as an opportunity to make a sale. You take control and then subtly guide the interviewer into making you a job offer. Your main goal during the interview is to transform yourself in the eyes of the interviewer from a total stranger to someone that his company must buy.

Listen actively

One of the greatest misconceptions about interviews is that it is the interviewee's moment in the spotlight where he can speak as much as he wants to about himself. On the contrary, active listening is twice as important as speaking in interviews. While a chatty candidate's enthusiasm to please the employer may seem amusing, it doesn't always result to a productive interview. Simply put, it's not about how much you say but how much value your words contain.

Listen closely to what the interviewer says about his business/organization. Your responses must be based according to his company's needs. This way, you turn from being a job applicant to a partner who's eager to share ideas and solutions.

Be on the lookout for conversation builders
From time to time, the interviewer will say some things that you can use to build an interesting conversation.

Example:

Interviewer: "The low inventory turnover is one of our biggest problems."

Applicant: "I understand completely. I've had experience in finding solutions for low inventory turnover in my previous position. Exactly what type of problems are you facing at the moment?"

Mirror
When you listen, don't just sit there like a cold marble statue. This would embarrass or offend your interviewer. Worse, it might send the message that you're not that interested in the job after all. Respond through your body language. Nod in agreement from time to time. That said, don't exaggerate your responses by agreeing to every single thing that the interviewer says. You must have your own opinions. Even so, restrain yourself and put your opinions on

hold long enough to hear the interviewer out. You may not 100% agree with what the interviewer is saying, but play your cards right by finding a common ground and taking it from there.

Example:

Interviewer: "I think _____ is highly important. To accomplish this, we must use Approach A or Approach C."

Applicant: "I certainly agree that _____ is of primary importance. And I also favor approach C. While I can see the advantages of using Approach A, have you considered trying Approach B?"

Interviewer: "Why?"

Applicant: "Well, based from my experience, one of the greatest advantages of Approach B is…"

Lean forward slightly or sit at the edge of your seat to communicate to the interviewer that you find the exchange stimulating. Practice the art of mirroring the interviewer's message. This means that you match his/her tone. When he's excited about something, reflect his enthusiasm. When he adopts a serious tone while discussing a certain topic, reflect his seriousness.

Important: Limit your use of mirroring techniques, especially when it comes to mimicking your interviewer's body language.

It's true that mimicry may serve as a social glue that can assist in the promotion of rapport between human beings. In fact, years of research has proved that generally, subtly mirroring another person's tone, vocabulary, words, posture, and gestures can make you seem more likable to that individual. However, more than one recent study by psychological researchers reveal that when it comes to job interviews, mimicry must be kept to a minimum, especially when there is more than one interviewer.

In an experiment done by scientists from University of California, San Diego, several mock interviews were recorded. In the interviews, some of the participants mimicked the interviewers' gestures while others did not. After this, the scientists asked judges to watch the videos and measure the interviewees' level of competence, likeability, and credibility. The result? The judges found the candidates who kept mirroring to a minimum to be more competent, credible, and likeable.

A similar study was conducted by a team of experts at Texas Tech and Drew Universities. According to the study, mirroring can have negative effects on an applicant's success. This is because humans mimic not only positive gestures but also negative gestures as well. In other words, if your interviewer happens to find you less likeable or if he's just having a bad day, mirroring his gestures, his facial expression, or his tone of voice will only cause you to send a negative message to his subconscious. You become a living mirror of his negative emotions. Seeing you reflect how he's feeling inside will only serve to reinforce his negative perception of you.

Therefore, use mirroring strategies sparingly. Instead, concentrate on using body language to convey confidence and enthusiasm. You already have a lot on your mind during an interview and this is one less thing that you should worry about.

Repeat and rephrase

Rephrasing is one way to prove to the interviewer that you've been listening to him attentively. Like mirroring, rephrasing must be kept to a minimum. Make sure you restate only the most important points to the interviewer.

Example:

"If I understand you correctly…"

"From what I understand, you're saying that..."

Remind the interviewer why you're there in the first place

This may seem a bit frustrating, but in case the interviewer comes unprepared, his rambling thoughts may lead the conversation into an unpredictable path that will hinder you from selling yourself most effectively. At this point, your job is to give him a little nudge back to the right direction.

Example: "I just can't tell you how excited I am to be here. I believe that what I have to offer could be of use to this company."

With a statement like this, you're placing the focus back on the reasons why you're the right person for the job.

You might come across an interviewer who likes to monopolize the conversation. Should you butt in? Definitely. How else would you be able to have the opportunity to sell yourself?

But how do you interrupt a talkative interviewer's monologue without seeming rude?

First, absorb what you can from the interviewer's words. What you're actually listening in for are conversation builders and opportunities to highlight your selling points. Once it comes out of your interviewer's non-stop mouth, pounce on it.

Example:

INTERVIEWER: "As I was saying, one of the biggest challenges in this business is to guarantee sufficient cash flow--"

APPLICANT: "Allow me to interrupt you for a second. What you're saying is just too interesting. Management of cash flow is actually one of my main areas of interest. I have a couple of fresh ideas which you might be interested in hearing and I can't wait to hear your thoughts on them..."

Another type of interviewer you might come across is the stressed out, overworked type. He/she may be distracted during the whole interview. He/she may even cut you short to answer phone calls. Instead of feeling indignant, express your sympathy. Then, use it as a way to bring up the value that you can add to the company.

Example:

"Wow, you really are very busy during this time of the year. I know what it's like and I can totally see why the company could use someone with my skills and experience."

This will direct the interviewer's attention back to you.

Remember: There are times when the job interviewing task falls on a chiefly technical person. When this happens, you get an interviewer who will lead the conversation into a discussion of technical matters. While it's important to demonstrate your technical know-how, it is also necessary to remember that this isn't all that your interviewer wants to know about you. Naturally, he'll also want to know what you would be like as an employee. Chances are, he may be having a hard time communicating what he really wants to ask you. The solution? Look for a way to connect your technical skills with your transferrable skills. Provide examples of situations where you used *both*.

Keep in mind the lessons that your high school teacher taught you

Whoever said that high school subjects have no practical application in real life wasn't familiar with the rules of successful interviews. Remember when your grammar school teacher kept hounding you about using a substantial topic sentence, an engaging introduction, and a powerful conclusion in your essays?

Well, you have to follow the same rules when answering interview questions.

Open with your topic sentence. Then, proceed with statements that support the topic sentence. Finally, end with a conclusion that summarizes your point.

Example:

"I understand that it's my job to find out and cater to our potential clients' needs, which will, in turn, enable me to <u>INCREASE</u> *the company's sales.* This is why I made it my business to help the company to *earn* _____ dollars in sales last quarter. I was able to *persuade* former clienteles such as _____ and _____ to *purchase* the company's most recent products. I also *secured* new clients such as _____ and _____. Moreover, I *collaborated* with _____ and _____ departments to help draw more attention to the company's flagship product, which is _____, and thus, maximizing its visibility to potential consumers. *Within one year of being in the company, I increased the company's sales by* _____ *% through diligence, social skills, salesmanship abilities, and by being a team player."*

Phrases that Keep the Ball Rolling
Using the following magic phrases will aid in maintaining the momentum of the conversation:

"I agree..."

"I can certainly relate..."

"That's interesting..."

"We should talk about..."

"Tell me more..."

"We should pursue that further..."

"That's also one of my biggest concerns..."

There are also phrases that could stop a conversation dead in its tracks. Here are a few examples of what you must avoid:

"Definitely not..."

"I absolutely disagree..."

"There is no way..."

"It's impossible..."

"It's final..."

"That's not how it should be done..."

Be on the lookout for 'Buy Signals'

You'll know an interviewer is interested in you when he starts using phrases such as the following:

"Sounds great."

"Interesting."

"I like that!"

Buy signals like these are signs that you've successfully caught your employer with your hook. Now it's time for you to reel him in, proverbially speaking. You do this by expounding on the idea that captured his interest. That said, unless they're really, really impressed, interviewers are rarely expressive. Often, their buy signals come in the form of a request for you to elaborate further on the topic.

Example:

"Can you tell me more about..."
"I'd like to hear more about..."
"Let's go back to..."
"Would you care to be more specific about..."
Now, most interviewees would dread the idea of being asked to speak more about a certain topic. Since you're reading this book, you shouldn't be feeling this way any longer! This is an indicator that you've hit the right button. But what is the correct way of expounding on an idea?

In marketing, a product's *features* refer to the characteristics of the product (ex: portable, compact, etc.) If you're a product, then your features are your skills (ex: great managerial skills, reliable, trustworthy, etc.) On the other hand, a product's *benefits* refer to the positive things that it can do for the user (ex:

portable, compact materials can be used while on the go and are easy to store.)

It's your *features* that will catch the interviewer's attention. To draw him in, you now have to present your *benefits*. In other words: *How can your skills make the employer's business/life more profitable/better?*

Example:

"I believe that the most important part of my position as an assistant manager is to *provide you* with more *time* to pursue higher responsibilities. My goal is to support you in the management of the store so you can have more valuable time in your hands."

Make a closing statement that closes the sale

You're playing the part of a salesman. This means you're not leaving the interview room without urging the employer to seal the deal.

Wrong: "So, did I get the job?"/"Did I do okay?"
This comes across as overly presumptuous, pathetic, and perhaps worst of all, needy. You're likely to end up with the standard dismissive response: "Don't call us. We'll call you."

Correct:

"Based on all that I've told you, don't you think I would be a great fit for the company?"

This part can be quite tricky. You need to make use of a closing statement that will actually extract a positive answer from the employer. To use or not to use closing statements like this will depend on how well you've established rapport with your interviewer and how effectively you were able to answer the interview questions. If you have a good feeling about the interview, proceed to prompt the employer into action. If not, follow a different route:

"Thank you so much for your time, Mr./Mrs./Ms. _____. It has been great pleasure and I do believe I have a great deal to offer to this institution. But please, if there's anything that I wasn't able to discuss to your satisfaction, do let me know. What could I tell you to encourage you to make a proposal?"

Keep in mind that it's not about pressuring the employer to make a decision on the spot. This is about increasing your chances of urging the employer to commit to you positively. Closing statements like these suggest a hint of urgency without the sense of impatience or desperation. It simply reminds the interviewer of your value.

Chapter 3: Experience Related Questions

What would your boss say is an area you could improve on?

Question Type:

Background and Personality

Question Analysis:

The interviewer will use this question to assess how well the candidate embraces critical feedback. No matter how strong a performance review might be, most managers will offer up at least one area for improvement. The interviewer is looking for the candidate to be candid about an area for improvement and discuss how they are taking action. Ideally, your response would discuss an area you are new to and investing time to improve.

What to Avoid:

You should avoid criticizing your boss's judgement. A response such as "my boss told me I need to pay better attention to detail but I disagree with her assessment" will not go over well with the interviewer.

It will portray you as someone who is not receptive to critical feedback from superiors. You should also avoid saying something such as "my boss has never suggested an area for improvement." Remember that this question is a hypothetical. If your boss has not provided critical feedback, then you can still come up with your own area for self-improvement. Finally, you should avoid discussing areas that would be concerning to the interviewer. If you are interviewing for a sales position and you mention that you need to become better at communicating with customers, you will create a cause for concern.

Example Response:

My boss would say I could get better at recognizing when my work load is at full capacity and delegating work. I recently moved into a supervisor role, but I still put too much on my own plate which causes me unnecessary stress. When tasks and projects come up I tend to gravitate toward taking full ownership over them instead of working with my team to find out who is in the best position to do the work.

I recently implemented weekly update meetings with my team so that we can run through everyone's workload and availability. These meetings have helped me identify opportunities to delegate project work throughout our team to create a better balance for everyone.

Why is there a gap in your employment history? (if applicable)

Question Type:

Background and Personality

Question Analysis:

If the interviewer asks this question they are looking for an upfront and honest response. The best way to approach this question largely depends on the reason for the gap. If you were laid off, you should provide some details of the situation and discuss why the company decided to reduce headcount. If you took a leave of absence, you can explain the situation from a high level but there is no need to go into too many personal details. For example, "I had a health scare I needed to resolve" or "a family member became ill and needed my full attention" is enough detail. You should try to incorporate positive items in your employment history before and after the gap. It is also beneficial if you can discuss your ambitious intentions during the gap period.

What to Avoid:

You should avoid getting defensive with your response. Your answer should not be centered around any excuses with past employment. Whether it was a result of a prior job or a personal reason that resulted in the gap, you should avoid going into too many unnecessary details.

Example Response:

When I previously worked at XYZ Company, they unexpectedly lost their largest customer and needed to take drastic action to stay in business. 25% of the sales force was laid off including most members on my team. It felt like a punch in the gut, but I understood the Company did not have much of a choice.

As I considered my next steps, I decided that it was important not to jump at the first opportunity but instead take the time to find the right fit for my career. I treated the job search like a full-time position, spending most of my days making new connections and setting up coffee or lunch meetings with business contacts in the area. I also made time to take a two-week online sales training course I had been interested in for over a year. After 4 months of networking and consideration, I decided to accept a position for a territory sales manager at XYZ Company.

What are three skills all professionals in this field should possess?

Question Type:

Industry and Company Specific

Question Analysis:

The interviewer will likely ask this question using the name of the profession such as "What are three skills all accountants should possess?" You should be prepared to discuss skills that are highly relevant to your profession and align closely with the job description. The interviewer is typically looking for the candidate to hone in on certain skill sets that are a must for the profession (i.e. excellent verbal communication skills for a nurse). The following skills are highly relevant to nearly all professions: Effective communicator, attention to detail, excellent planner, and strong time management.

What to Avoid:

Your answer should avoid overly generic skills that are presumed for all professionals such as "hard worker." Your answer should also not be a laundry list of skills. Be sure to discuss how each skill benefits the professional in their respective field.

Example Response:

(Example response is for accountants)

Successful accountants focus on attention to detail to ensure their work is complete and accurate. We work in a profession where small mistakes can have profound consequences. Attention to detail in this profession means fully understanding the scope of the work and expectations before completing it. It also means critical self-reviews before finalizing our work.

Accountants should also be excellent at planning their work at a micro and macro level. Time management is essential to staying on track and meeting deadlines.

Finally, all successful accountants should be effective communicators. Whether it is meeting with a boss, collaborating with team members, or discussing an issue with a client, accountants need to have strong written and verbal communication skills.

What was something you did not like about your previous (or current) position?

Question Type:

Background and Personality

Question Analysis:

This can be a tricky question because candidates are often tempted to heavily criticize their previous job or employer, but this can reflect poorly on the candidate's own personality and professionalism. You should discuss why you did not prefer a certain management style, a team dynamic, or a job limitation from a professional perspective.

What to Avoid:

Unless something drastic happened (such as fraud or harassment), it is important to stay away from character attacks or interoffice drama because the interviewer may associate it with your own personality. It is also wise to avoid criticism of common challenges that occur in most work environments such as "too much stress," "long hours," or "a demanding boss." These answers may lead to the interviewer questioning whether the candidate can handle adversity which will come up often in most positions.

Example Response:

Overall, I was really satisfied with my previous position. I worked with a great team and grew as a professional. I do wish I would have had more leadership opportunities in my previous role. The company was traditional in the sense that most project work was initiated and micro managed by the company's leadership. I thrive in an environment that offers leadership opportunities for all employees.

Question Type:

Behavioral

Question Analysis:

The interviewer will use this question to assess the candidate's team working capabilities. They want to know that the candidate possesses sufficient emotional intelligence to successfully adapt to the various personalities of co-workers. You should discuss an example that shows your ability to effectively communicate with a differing personality to achieve the desired results.

What to Avoid:

You should avoid criticizing a team member's personality. You should also avoid examples of working around another team member or excluding them from the work. The interviewer wants to see that you are able to adapt to various situations to find positive ways to work together with other team members.

Example Response:

S/T: Last year I lead a system implementation project with four other team members. I scheduled weekly update meetings to discuss the status of the project and to encourage collaboration on technical issues we were encountering. I noticed that one of our team members was extremely quiet during our team meetings, but he would often email me afterwards with excellent insight and ideas about the issues we had just discussed in the team setting. Not hearing his ideas until after our meetings was hurting our team collaboration. It was also inefficient for me to communicate his ideas back to the team versus all of us discussing them during the meetings.

A: I looked into his experience and employment history and noted that he had just graduated from college and joined the company one month prior. Instead of talking with him about the issue during the next team meeting, I decided to schedule a one-on-one meeting. I explained to him that I was a bit nervous and shy when I first started with the company and that it was completely normal. I also tried to boost his confidence by explaining how valuable his follow up ideas had been toward the project. I explained the benefits of speaking up during team meetings but made sure not to make him feel too much pressure.

R: Over the course of the next few weeks we all started to observe him grow more comfortable with sharing his input during the team meetings. While he may be disposed to a more reserved personality, the ability to acknowledge that and work with him enabled us to use his talents to add more value to our team.

Do you prefer working in a team setting or independently?

Question Type:

Background and Personality

Question Analysis:

This question can be tricky to some candidates because it sounds as if the interviewer is asking them to take up a definitive preference for one setting over the other. However, most positions require candidates to work both independently and within a group. Unless the job description explicitly calls for working independently or in a team setting at all times, the best response is to explain that you are comfortable working in both environments.

What to Avoid:

It is okay if you prefer working independently over working with a team or vice versa but you should avoid making a bold preference in your answer. The interviewer may view your strong preference as a sign that you are weak in the other area.

Example Response:

It largely depends on the situation. Some projects and tasks are best accomplished through team work and collaboration while others are more effectively completed through independent work. I have a do-whatever-it-takes mindset and feel comfortable as a team player collaborating in a group setting but can also buckle down and work independently when needed.

Did you get along with your prior boss?

Question Type:

Background and Personality

Question Analysis:

The interviewer will use this question to get a better sense of the candidate's ability to work well with superiors. The interviewer wants to know whether you create or burn bridges. You will usually only hurt yourself by heavily criticizing your previous or current boss. Unless your boss did something highly unethical or illegal, you should focus on a positive answer.

What to Avoid:

You should avoid personal insults and character attacks when describing your previous boss. If your answer is strongly critical of your boss, the interviewer will likely view you as someone who does not respect superiors or get along well with co-workers.

Example Response:

I enjoyed working for my former boss. She never let her team get bored with their work. I was always presented with new challenges and learning opportunities. She also placed a strong emphasis on team communication and had an open-door policy for new ideas. Her management style helped me grow as a professional.

What type of salary are you seeking?

Question Type:

Background and Personality

Question Analysis:

Unlike question #69, you should not offer up a dollar amount in your response to this question. Instead, focus your answer on your enthusiasm for the position and desire to receive a competitive offer. Effective salary negotiators typically avoid being the first one to throw out a figure.

What to Avoid:

You should avoid discussing a specific desired salary figure in your response.

Example Response:____

I am excited about the opportunities that come with this position but have not focused on a specific salary figure. If you were to offer me the job, I would hope to get an offer that is competitive with the salary range for this position while taking into consideration my experience and skillset.

Tell me about a time you had to deal with a difficult co-worker. What was the outcome?

Question Type:

Behavioral

Question Analysis:

The interviewer will ask this question to assess the candidate's ability to manage conflict in the work setting. They want to know that the candidate will not ignite a conflict but will also not run away from it. Your answer should demonstrate that you are able to work through a disagreement in a professional manner and find resolution toward a common goal.

What to Avoid:

When discussing why a co-worker was difficult to work with you should avoid insulting them or getting into too many personal details about their character. Your answer should focus more on the resolution than the individual. You should also avoid discussing tedious or irrelevant conflicts such as "she always eats my lunch from the refrigerator."

Example Response:____

S/T: In my prior role as a financial analyst, I was tasked with testing our key financial reports when updates were made to our ERP system. After a significant update, I noted that one of our accounts receivable reports was broken. The data it produced was critical to our quarterly reporting package which was due in three days. The systems analyst who managed the technical side of the financial reports was not responsive to my emails or phone calls and when I stopped by his desk to let him know the importance of fixing the report, he blew me off.

A: I was frustrated with his response and lack of interest in helping our team get the report fixed. However, I remained calm and requested a meeting with him to sit down for fifteen minutes to help clear the air. He apologized for not being attentive to our request and explained that he had five different projects going on and was working thirteen-hour days to keep up. We both decided it was best to schedule a meeting with him and his manager to explain our team's urgent situation and help prioritize his time.

R: After meeting with his manager, she was able to shuffle around some of his project work to ensure our report was fixed on time. They were both appreciative that I took the time to sit down with them to explain the situation and find a solution that worked well for everyone.

Chapter 4: Education Questions

The more recent your graduation, the more intense the interest will be in your education. Because your work experience may be limited, expect to be quizzed for clues to your interests and motivation. For example, how you chose your college and your major (or why you switched), what your extracurricular activities were, any internships you had, and any future career plans (or why you didn't graduate or attend college). Of course, the more your college days recede into the distant past, the less interest there will be in your education. The interviewer can then focus his or her eagle eyes on your work experience.

Why did you choose your major and minor?

These courses were relevant to my chosen career and provided a solid foundation for it.

What the interviewer is asking/looking for: The interviewer wants a sense of your thinking process and interests, and this seems like a good place to start.

Good answer: Give a reasonable reason why. In many jobs, such as computer programming or engineering, it's expected that you majored in computer science or engineering. In other jobs, a wide variety of majors is found in employees. Or perhaps you are passionately interested in the subject, even if it's not "practical." Even if you majored in the Greek and Roman classics, philosophy, or Far East studies, and are interviewing for a job where this is not remotely relevant, be prepared to defend your choice without being defensive. But regardless, be ready to discuss the skills you learned, whether it's researching, writing, communication, or analytical skills.

Bad answer: An answer that shows lack of thought, laziness, or lack of direction. "Because I had to choose something," "It was cool" or "an easy A," or because your parents insisted, your friends were majoring in it, or the workload was lighter than other majors.

What extracurricular activities did you take part in?

I was on my college debate team, arguing topics from ethical to economic issues—and it was a good preparation for my business career.

What the interviewer is asking/looking for: The interviewer wants more of a sense of your interests and how you occupy your leisure time. They hope that you are a well-rounded person who devotes energy and time to something besides your studies.

Good answer: Show that you were interested and involved in things outside school hours—the more these are job-related or show traits the job requires, the better. Perhaps you worked on your college newspaper or yearbook as a prelude to your career in public relations or magazine, newspaper, or book publishing. Or your college basketball games taught you the importance of teamwork and listening to your coach. If you were busy working to pay for college or family bills, with little or no time for clubs or sports, don't be afraid to admit this, noting how you got a jump start on the work world and responsibility over your peers.

Bad answer: Anything that smacks of being a couch potato who simply watched TV or goofed off with your frat buddies after (or instead of) your classes.

Did you have an internship or a cooperative work-study program? If so, what did you learn?

My work-study program taught me a great deal about the field and valuable skills like working with others or research skills, which tie into the job I am seeking.

What the interviewer is asking/looking for: An internship (paid or unpaid) or cooperative work-study program is an excellent way to demonstrate work experience while still in college, differentiate yourself from your peers, and show seriousness of intent.

Good answer: Even if yours was of the coffee-fetching, photocopying, ho-hum variety, highlight the good points, like the chance to actually see and hear how the work was done and network with colleagues.

Bad answer: Bad-mouthing your internship or work-study program, having one in an utterly unrelated field (which makes the interviewer wonder about your real interest in this job), or acting like a smug know-it-all because of your experience.

An internship or cooperative work-study program isn't just a great way to land work experience that looks good on your resume—it may lead to a job. Employers hired 38 percent of their interns and almost 51 percent of their work-study students, a survey of 360 employers by NACE found.

Why are you looking for a job in a field other than in your major?

I enjoyed a volunteer work in this field so much I wanted to switch.

What the interviewer is asking/looking for: The interviewer wants to know your thinking behind your change of direction. Changes of direction are common among young job-seekers—and many older ones as well—but he or she wants to be convinced this job in this field is right for you, now.

Good answer: Make a case on how you looked more carefully at your career goals and the job you are interviewing for is more suitable for various reasons. Perhaps it's a fast-growing field with more opportunity - and jobs for medieval French literature majors were limited. Focus squarely on this job, and relate the skills you developed in your major and any work experience to it as much as possible.

Bad answer: A vague response that reveals you haven't given much thought to your change of direction, and perhaps are taking a scattershot approach to your career planning.

Name an accomplishment during your college years that you are proud of...

I captained the debate team and led it to victory.

What the interviewer is asking/looking for: The interviewer is looking for evidence that you devoted time and energy to setting a positive goal and achieving it, and demonstrated traits or skills which hopefully you will carry over to your career.

Good answer: Anything from an extracurricular activity (at college or outside of college) to a job or volunteer work that shows traits or skills in demand in the work world, such as leadership, initiative, or communication skills. Perhaps you started a campus business making T-shirts, sponsored a child overseas with your parents, or were a candy striper at the local hospital.

Bad answer: Stunned silence, a fumbled response, or anything that tempts the interviewer to think your college years were one long spring break (or that the movie Animal House was modeled after your college experience).

Be sure to dress appropriately and act professionally during the interview, even if the company has lots of young, casually dressed employees. Young job-seekers often are casually dressed in T-shirts, flip-flops, and shorts; answer their cell phones; and pepper interviews with words like "cool," "awesome," "you know," and "like," hiring managers complain.

If you had it to do over, what college courses would you take?

Marketing and public speaking.

What the interviewer is asking/looking for: The interviewer hopes your answer will show your understanding of what the job will require, and include a relevant course or two.

Good answer: Naming courses relevant to the job at hand, in terms of knowledge or skills. For example, marketing, statistics, journalism, or public speaking courses are good answers, if you can make a case the job requires this subject matter or skills.

Bad answer: Anything that shows a complete change of direction from the major you chose, or courses irrelevant to the job at hand, like Chinese art history or philosophy.

Why did you choose your college?

Because it offered a particularly strong program in my field of interest.

What the interviewer is asking/looking for: He or she wants to see anything that shows seriousness of purpose and solid decision-malting ability.

Good answer: Perhaps your school features outstanding professors with time for their students.

Bad answer: Anything that confirms the interviewer's worst fears that you chose your school for the chance to party nonstop without your parents around, because it was the only school that accepted you, or you were forced into it because your father or mother went there.

How do you keep learning? (Or: How do you stay informed?)

I read a local newspaper and at least one business publication, such as The New York Times every day.

What the interviewer is asking/looking for: The interviewer wants to know if you are a professional with an inquiring, curious mind who strives to keep up with information and update your skills. Continuing education has never been more important than today, since technology and globalization have changed every industry.

Good answer: You regularly read trade publications in your field to keep on top of what's happening in your industry. Perhaps you also belong to a professional association, attend its conferences, meetings, or workshops and read its newsletter, take a class to learn a new skill or even a graduate degree like an MBA at night, or teach a class or speak at conferences in your field.

Bad answer: Anything that implies you stopped learning when you finished school, perhaps have not cracked a book open since then, have closed your mind to new things, and get all your information from TV.

Why didn't you finish college? (Or: Why didn't you go to college?)

I had to drop out due to lack of money but I'm willing to finish it within a few years.

What the interviewer is asking/looking for: The interviewer hopes you had a solid reason, as opposed to lack of interest in learning or discipline.

Good answer: If there was any extenuating circumstance, like needing to support your family, or health problems, by all means say so. If you are currently completing your college degree, or plan to, admit it, since this shows you realize its importance. Many people who didn't finish college, stopped after a while, or didn't attend right after high school go later in life when the timing is better, and sometimes go on to earn graduate degrees, including law and medicine.

Bad answer: An answer that shows insufficient interest in learning, displays the inability to focus or discipline yourself for very long, or leads the interviewer to wonder if you knew why then or even now.

Why did you leave college and return later?

I chose to work full-time for a while to gain solid work experience and money to complete my degree.

What the interviewer is asking/looking for: The interviewer hopes to hear any good explanation for your stop-out.

Good answer: Perhaps you traveled, which you found an invaluable learning experience, devoted time to caring for your family, or simply needed to explore your interests and focus your goals more clearly.

Bad answer: You can't articulate a reason for either why you left or why you returned, or say you simply wanted to party a lot.

Summary

You've learned your college days can reveal a lot about you, so treat them as you would your work experience.

Be ready to give examples of how you demonstrated communication skills, leadership, a strong work ethic, and other things that employers value highly. Don't be surprised if your employer wants to know how you keep learning, even now.

• Tie in subjects you studied, your accomplishments, and extracurricular activities to the job at hand as much as you can.

• Talk about what you learned from internships and part-time, summer, and work-study jobs.

• Dress, speak, and act professionally in the interview.

• Give a good reason for bad grades or leaving/ not attending college, if that's the case.

Chapter 5: What You Will Bring to The Position

Once they have gotten what a sense of your personality is like, they will then start to try and investigate why they should pick you over all the other candidates. You made it past the point of being a qualified person on an individual level through your own character and experiences. This is your chance to shine and set yourself apart from all other candidates.

Remember to not simply memorize the answers that we are giving you. This only makes it harder on you in the actual interview. The point of the example answer is just so you can get a sense of a realistic and solid response. Keep it personalized to you, because setting yourself apart from the rest is of utmost importance!

"Tell me where you see yourself in the future (six months/five years/ten years from now)."

This is a common question that interviewers might even ask right at the beginning of the interview. This is a question that will be inclusive of all aspects of your life. Where do you see yourself in your career? What about your family life? In your personal goals? They don't just want to hear, "Hopefully working here!" They want to know that you are thinking about your future and that you have a plan. They want to see if they will fit into your plan. You might consider saying something like this when that question is asked:

"In six months, I hope that I am settled into a position and in a place where I can focus on really improving my skills. At the same time, I want to ensure that I'm doing my best to also consistently check in with my personal goals. Eventually, I hope to achieve a position of employment where I'm making a comfortable amount of money. I know the future is always changing so I'm also excited to see what surprises the future might bring me!"

"Why should we hire YOU?"

Every job will have several people applying for the position. All of the questions asked so far likely helped them to realize whether or not they want to hire you based on your experience and so on, but other candidates have probably fit the criteria they have too. Why should they hire you and not someone else? What stands out about you that will make you the best candidate? This is going to be specific to you. Perhaps you have a valuable skill that's hard to come by. Maybe it's something in your history that makes you unique. What are the qualities that really set you apart from the competition?

"I believe I'm the right pick because of my set of skills and experiences that I have had. I not only do what I'm asked, but I make sure to go above and beyond and deliver something greater than what I was asked. I take pride in my work, even if it is not a task I am particularly passionate about at the moment. I will always deliver work with exceptional detail and attention to the things that matter the most."

"What about this position makes you want to work here? Why do you want to get hired?"

The "Why do you want to work here" question is always going to be in the interview. It's not a trick question! Your interviewer will legitimately want to know why it is that you chose them. The obvious answer is, "Because I need a job and I saw you were hiring. I want money." This is usually the first thing that we will consider when applying to a job. While this might be the truth, try to honestly remember why it is that you want this position and not another. Have your reason prepared before even making your way into the interview. When you can give substantial answers based directly on their mission statement, then that will give you a big advantage.

"I want to work here because I have always been a lifelong supporter of this company. I have frequented the stores and I understand what the clientele is like. Not only do I think this will help me to be more passionate and dedicated to my work, but I think it helps because I will be more knowledgeable about what the business actually stands for. When I have this connection to the workplace, it is easier to go above and beyond because I have the confidence to know what my talents are and how the company will benefit from them."

"What do you know about us? How would you describe our company?"

This is a question that will require a lot of research! Make sure you Google your company before the interview. Don't just go to their site either. Read reviews if it is a service-based place or a retail location. If it is a huge company, look up news articles that might focus on them. Go on forums and see if anyone else has worked there and what their stories are like. The more you know about them, the easier this will be. Make sure that you list out what their services are, what their employees do, and what their mission statement is. This is a specific question, so make sure that your answer is based specifically on the company that you are interviewing for!

"What unique skills do you have that only apply to this specific position?"

This is another specific one that will apply only to the position that you are interviewing for. If you are looking to get hired as a front desk clerk, then you would want skills involving talking to people, handling requests, taking messages, making appointments, and other clerical work. If you are applying to be a construction worker, then you'll need to make sure that you can lift heavy things, operate heavy machinery, and have basic construction knowledge.

Whenever you are applying for a job, they'll usually have a list of objectives in their job description. Make sure that you study these. They will give you the exact insight needed to understand what unique skills that you have specifically for this job. They might have a job description that says things like:

Must be proficient in Word

Have excellent communication skills

Punctual and reliable

And so on.

Remember them, and when you get to your interview, you will be able to state them in your own way. Discuss your technical skills on the computer. Talk about how you can communicate. Give examples of how you are reliable. When you bring up keywords that they're looking for, they're going to be more likely to keep you in the back of their mind when making the final decision.

"What are you hoping to accomplish in this position?"

This is a seemingly obvious question, but it can actually catch a lot of people off guard. It seems to be one of the most obvious questions that can actually reveal a deeper truth about someone who might be applying for the job. There are a few ways that you can answer this. You can discuss how you would like to move up to a higher position if that is something you believe to be an option. Alternatively, you can discuss how you hope to gain valuable skills if it is not a position that offers a lot of growth.

"I hope while I'm working here, if hired, of course, that I can discover new skills that I may have and improve on things I need to work on while also helping the business thrive. I know the things that I need to improve on, and I have goals for myself. I think this company's goals and the goals I have for myself line up well together so that we can both mutually benefit from what I might experience here."

"How many responsibilities do you feel comfortable having at a time?"

This is a good question to help them to determine whether or not you are a multi-tasker. Some people are comfortable handling just one thing at a time, while others can handle several different things at once. Do your best to answer honestly because even if you struggle to do several things at once, that doesn't mean you're not a good employee! We all have a different pace for completing tasks so ensure that you are being honest with them. Can you handle several projects, or are you someone that works at a slower pace on one thing at a time? While you can easily lie and say that you can take on a bunch of things at once, you are just setting yourself up to make things more challenging later on. Be honest!

"I am pretty good with time management, so I don't mind taking on a few things at once. I will always try to complete tasks much faster than I say I will so that I can go above and beyond. I don't take on too much at once because I know my limits and do my best to avoid feeling overwhelmed or burnt out."

"Can you adjust quickly to a rapidly changing environment? Would you be able to change your plans if something unexpected happened?"

There may be a time when your employer has to send you to a different location, or perhaps they need you to work in a different department, depending on your skills and the versatility of management. It is up to you, then, to make sure that you know how to adapt should a situation like this occur. Be honest with them and let them know if you are going to be able to quickly adapt to situations like this if that's what you have to do later on.

"I have no problem trying new things. I appreciate having a set schedule so that I know what needs to be done, but when things change, it can just make work feel more exciting, making going to work more enjoyable. I'm not concerned about my abilities to adapt should there be a situation when I need to quickly adjust to change."

"What strong organizational skills do you have?"

Being organized is incredibly important. They can simply ask, do you have this skill, or this skill, or this skill, and so on, but instead, they are leaving this question for you to fill in the blanks. Rather than blatantly stating that you are detail oriented, punctual, and so on, put an emphasis on sharing your actual steps to become organized so that they can have a better sense of whether or not you are really someone with a great set of organization skills.

"I think organization is incredibly important in order to avoid any issues that might arise during any given project. To get organized, I first make a list of all the tasks that I need to do. From there, I will prioritize them by importance and separate them by how much time they will take and look at ways that I might be able to complete two tasks simultaneously. From there, I do my best to adhere to timelines, always giving myself a little extra time to account for any incidents that might occur!"

"If you were part of a group project, and you started to feel as though other members weren't pulling their weight, how would you handle this situation?"

This can be a frustrating feeling. Maybe there's a group project that includes five people, but there's that one guy who is not pulling his weight. Alternatively, perhaps everyone else is doing all the work and not letting you have the chance to thrive. Your interviewer wants to know how you would handle it if you found yourself in either of these scenarios.

"First, I would address whether there are issues within myself. Am I not delegating tasks properly? Is there a lack of communication? I would ensure I was doing everything I could on my part, and then address issues within the group. I would do it one on one and pull people aside to have personal conversations about the project. If I felt like I wasn't having the opportunity to pull my weight and others were too controlling or were doing the work for me, I would take the same steps."

"What is a strong value that you have that is only related to a working environment?"

When we think of values, we might first think of religion, politics, or philosophy. You won't need to think of this for a question about your working values, however. They want to know what is important to you. How would you describe your work ethic? What is something that you always remind yourself when the going gets tough at work? This is another question specific to you, and there are a few ways you can answer. Here is one of them:

"One value that's important to me is persistence. Sometimes things don't go as planned, and you might have moments of failure, but I always remind myself to try again. If something consistently is not working, then I'll look for a different way to solve the problem. The more I focus on getting back on my feet and continuing the fight, the easier it is to achieve my goals. Even if I fail nine times, the 10th time might be the time I succeed, so it's always important for me to continue on."

"What traits do you think an employee in this specific position should have?"

This is an important question because it will be specific to the employees and what you know about the company already. It shows them what you really think that you will be doing in the position if hired. The question is not just about you, it's about the position. You should put yourself in the perspective of the person conducting the interview, making it easier to see what they might be looking for. When you can do this, it becomes easier to know what a good answer would be. You might base this on a job description that you saw, or it could simply be something that you gathered as you discussed different things throughout the interview. Your response might be something like this:

"I think that it's important for an employee in this position to be reliable. There are several people depending on them, and it seems as though there will be some high-pressure scenarios. If they can't be trusted professionally and personally, then that can put a wedge in the working environment."

"Can you sell me the chair that you are sitting on at the moment?"

This is a question that might be specific to those who are interviewing for a sales position. Even if you won't be working with sales, numbers, or customers at all, it can still be a question that pops up. It is one that will show how well you can try and persuade someone. Are you a good schmoozer? Do you have a creative mindset that helps you to see the benefits even in something as mundane as a chair? They will ask questions like this especially if you are in sales, but the question might differ in how it is presented. They might say something like, "Sell me this pencil", or ask you to sell another object that's around. Your sales pitch might look like this:

"This chair is great for anyone who is looking to sit down. We all could use a break, and when we do decide to get that moment of rest, then this chair is going to be your top choice. It has a cushioned top that makes it comfortable for your bottom, especially for those sitting for long periods of time. It has features where you can adjust the height of the chair, so anyone can benefit from it. Not only does it have great comfort features, but it's aesthetically pleasing as well. Why don't you give it a try for yourself?"

"Is it more important for people to like you in a managerial position, or for people to fear you?"

This is a common question, especially if you are going to be interviewing for a managerial position. It's a frequent discussion of whether or not a manager is supposed to be feared or if they should be liked. Do you want to be the boss that's popular with everyone or is it more important that they become obedient and respect your authority? The best way to answer this is that you should be right in the middle of both.

Chapter 6: Questions on Salary, Promotion and Benefits

How much was your last salary?

Most times, this question is hardly asked during job interviews. However, it is exclusively for people whose curriculum vitae show that they have been working. This is why this question is not asked to job seekers whose application packages show that they are fresh or new in the labor market. If the above question is asked, it is expected that the job you applied for should have higher and better prospects than the past ones. This means that the salary of the prospective job should be higher than your past salaries. If the difference is too wide, you may be considered under qualified for the job. You will be considered overqualified for the job if the salary of your past job is also higher than that of the job you applied for. But the exact difference, most likely, will be unknown to you since you know of the past salary alone. If you had/have a job with a good salary, mention the amount. Do not exaggerate or inflate your past salary because you may not have sufficient evidence, especially bank documents, to defend your false claim, if it is requested. Besides, some employers confirm their applicants' claims on salary prior to making a job offer. However, if your last salary is far below your salary expectation from the prospective job, politely appeal to the interviewer to wave the question aside.

Sample Answers

I am a fresh graduate. So, I have not been on salary as an employee.

I will crave your indulgence to wave this question aside because I am more concerned about the future than the past.

About how much do you expect to be paid as salary?

Try as much as you can to find the salary the organization is will be willing to pay if you are offered an appointment. Your ability to achieve this will help you not to overprice or underprice when you are asked this question. If, however, you were unable to find the salary structure of the organization and the amount the organization will be willing to pay if you are offered the appointment, you should apply caution in answering this question. The first caution to apply is to avoid mentioning anything about compensation or remuneration, before the question is asked. If salary-related issue should arise, let it be raised by the interviewer. Do not be in a haste in responding to this question. You should not give a specific answer to this question because the amount you mention may be too high or too low. In other words, you may overprice or underprice. You may not be considered for the job if the amount you mention is too high, as the employer may be afraid that you cannot be at home with the organization with the amount it can afford to pay. You may also be rejected on the ground that your standard is below that of the company, if the amount you mention is too low. One of the best approaches to answering this question is to give an open and unspecific answer. Another approach is to tell the interviewer that you have insufficient information to estimate your salary. If, however, you belong to a professional body that has a standard for the remuneration of different categories of its members, you can cite their recommendation/standard. The sample answers below reflect these categories of answers.

Sample Answers

I believe the salaries of your employees are determined by your corporate policy, and accepting your policy is a requisite for being an employee of your organization.

All other things equal, I know that the salary of an employee is determined by a variety of factors. This includes the value/worth of the employee, the status of the organization and the responsibilities and challenges of the job. I do not have enough information to comment on the salary, as I know of the first factor only - my value.

I am a member of the Institute of Chartered Accountants. The institute specifies that members who have my qualifications should be paid a minimum of Nabc,000 per annum. I expect that my salary should be within that range.

Is salary among the factors that determine the satisfaction you derive from a job?

Sample Answer

Though my salary has a role to play in making me happy in a job, it is not the most important thing to me about work. I am more interested in the career prospects of the job and its impact on my personal development.

How often do you expect increase in your salary?

Sample Answer

I believe this would be determined by a number of factors. This includes the policy of the company, my productivity in the organization and the overall success of the company.

How would you justify your salary?

Sample Answer

I expect to be paid from the money I make for the company, and I know that the organization will remain in existence only when the employees generate more money than they are paid. I will justify my income by ensuring that my services to the company surpass my remuneration.

What are your expectations if you are hired?

This question is not as simple as it appears to be. Just as you (should) have some expectations from the job you applied for and your prospective employer, the organization also has its expectations from you. However, you should choose a job because of your expectations from it but justify your interest in the job by emphasising the interest and expectations of the prospective employer. The expectations organizations are delighted with are employees' contributions to their success. Hence, do not say, "I expect the company to be prompt in the payment of salary". Also do not say, "I hope the company will soon increase my salary". You should also avoid saying, "I expect to be promoted very soon". Also avoid saying, "I hope the company will sponsor my vacations". No organization will offer you an appointment because of your expectations from it. Every prospective employer's interest in a job seeker is determined by its expectations - the value the job seeker will add to its organization. This is the area your answer should focus.

Sample Answers

I expect to be an invaluable asset to your organization if I am offered an appointment.

I hope to assist the company to the best of my ability in achieving her organizational goals.

If the interviewer insists on knowing your expectations from the job which will profit you, you should tell him about what you hope to profit from the job if you get the appointment. The expectation should have long term significance. Such question may be, **"Do you have other expectations from this job?"**

Sample Answer

I hope this job will afford me the opportunity to advance my career, if I get the appointment.

How soon do you hope to be promoted?
Sample Answer

I believe that my promotion will be determined by the policy of the company. I also know that my performance also has a role to play in earning my promotion because I will not be qualified for promotion until I am overqualified for the position I occupy.

Has your salary been delayed before?

Sample Answer

My past employers were very prompt in payment.

Has your salary ever been reduced?

Sample Answer

I am yet to have that experience in a place of work.

What would you do if your salary is delayed for any reason?

Sample Answer

It depends on the factor that is responsible for the delay. As an accountant, I will always know when the company is making profit and when it is having financial challenges. I am confident that the organization cannot afford to risk her reputation by owing the employees at a time it is making profit, and I also know that this organization has a reputation for accelerated growth.

Will you leave us if you get a better offer?

"**How soon would you join us if you are employed?**" Both questions are related, likewise their answers. Your answers to both questions should cohere. In the book, it was advised that you should be very careful with your answer because the prospective employer will not expect you to (promise to) start the new job immediately if you claimed to be working with an organization. It was also remarked that it is wrong to resign from a job without prior notification in order to join a new organization. In addition, it was noted that the interviewer may be afraid that you are not saying the truth or that you will frustrate their organizational activities with an abrupt resignation if you get a better job while with them, if you promise to start immediately. While answering the question, "**Will you leave us if you get a better offer?**", do not be in a haste with denying that you will not accept a better offer if it comes your way in the future. Remember, you aspire for progress, and one of the ways of achieving that is getting a job that is better than the one you applied for, even if you are offered appointment. You should be mindful of the fact that the interviewer is not ignorant of this. Consequently, exercise diplomacy and caution in answering this question.

Sample Answer

I desire progress in life. I also desire to advance my career. I know that I may not achieve that without getting a better job. However, I do not consider a job as a better one just because it has a higher remuneration. There are other conditions like job security and future prospects which are more important to me. However, I will not be in a haste to leave your organization so that I will not frustrate your activities. Since I will likely not spend the rest of my working years in your organization, I will respect your policy whenever I am about to resign.

Chapter 7: Managing Third-Party Recruiters

If you have not applied for jobs in a while, or if you are relatively new to the job market, then you need to pay close attention to this chapter.

Who Are Third-Party Recruiters?

Third-party recruiters (also known as headhunters, external recruiters, staffing or talent acquisition specialists, talent agents, among other titles) are professionals who companies hire to help them find candidates for open positions. The recruiters can either work for small or larger organizations or they can be independent contractors.

Regardless of where they work, it is important to understand that third-party recruiters work for the **companies they are helping**, not you. They have a financial interest in placing you, therefore, all of their advice to you must be taken with this in mind.

Well, one of the work-arounds for companies (other than ATS) is to have these external recruiters take care of this part of the process for them, so they don't have to comb through piles of résumés. Recruiters will do the initial screening of candidates and then present companies with several options, so the process is more manageable and efficient.

There are both positives and negatives with having third-party recruiters as part of your job search. Let's discuss both.

The Positives

1. If you connect with a recruiter and he or she winds up sending your résumé to a company, then you are substantially increasing your chances of your résumé being seen and then getting called for an interview.

2. A lot of times these recruiters have established relationships with the companies they represent which also means they have a good idea of what a particular hiring manager is looking for and what types of questions you can expect during the interview. This is incredibly valuable information.

3. Recruiters will help negotiate your salary and other benefits on your behalf so you do not need to speak with the company directly about any of those topics.

4. If you do not get an interview or an offer, and you enjoyed working with the recruiter, then you now have a new contact for possible future opportunities.

The Negatives

1. Recruiters only get paid (or earn a decent portion of their compensation) when you agree to a company's offer. In other words, they work on commission. Therefore, they may try to justify a weak dollar offer or a company's unwillingness to give you an extra week of vacation in the hopes that you'll sign your offer letter so they can get paid. Only <u>you</u> know what's really best for you.

2. Low barrier to entry. In today's world, almost anyone can be a recruiter and the market is, therefore, saturated with them. It can be a very cut-throat business when there are so many players which is why it's important to understand the potential pitfalls.

3. Some recruiters will use under-handed tactics to try and extract information from you that they can potentially use for their own purposes. More on this in a minute.

Over the years, I have heard (and personally experienced) many stories about questionable, rude, and/or unethical behavior toward job seekers by external recruiters. Recruiters who behave in this way are not worth your time. Only spend time working with the true professionals.

How to Connect with Recruiters

You can connect with recruiters in two ways: they reach out to you (usually via LinkedIn or your email) or you actively seek them out. Let's take each scenario separately.

They Reach out to You

This is common especially when your LinkedIn profile is updated. They are looking for potential candidates who may be willing to entertain the idea of switching companies.

If you are contacted by a recruiter, first make sure they want to discuss a **specific** position and you get the job description from them in writing before sending your résumé along. The reason this is important is because there are some recruiters out there who will "fish" for professionals to add into their databases and will lie about having an open position just to get your résumé and other details.

Story: Here is an actual email exchange to illustrate what I mean:

A recruiter sent an email with a brief, generic job description for a position in a job seeker's general geographic location. The company and location were not revealed.

Job Seeker: Thank you for the email. Can you tell me who the company is and the location?
No response from the recruiter. Job Seeker follows up with another email three days later.

Recruiter: This is a semi-confidential search in that we are disclosing the company once we have had a pre-qualification discussion via phone.

Job Seeker: I understand. I'd like to learn more. When is a good time to chat?

Recruiter: Are you actively looking?

Job Seeker: I'm keeping my options open. I'm free Thursday morning. Will that work?
No response from the recruiter.

No decent recruiter is going to drag his feet when there is an interested candidate for an open position. This exchange was highly suspect from the radio silence the recruiter gave the job seeker after the recruiter initially reached out. Fortunately for the job seeker, no real time was wasted and the recruiter only got the fact that the job seeker was interested. It doesn't matter because that recruiter has already proven not to be worth the job seeker's time.

Look out for nonsense like this.

There are right ways to build relationships and there are many wrong ways to go about it. Just be diligent and aware like you would when someone you don't know reaches out and starts asking for sensitive information.

You Reach out to Them

If you find you are having trouble searching on your own, either because of time or other constraints, then you can proactively reach out to recruiters as they may be able to help you.

There are also independent recruiters who are easily found on LinkedIn.

If they're smart, they will take your call and if they're professional, they'll be honest with you regarding whether they can ultimately help you then or in the future. In these cases, you will send them your résumé so they can get a clear understanding of your background and what you're looking to do next.

Note: In either case, never hand over your résumé unless you first have their agreement, in writing, that they will not send your résumé to any company without your written permission. Any good recruiter will understand this.

What's the big deal if they send out my résumé? It can't hurt, right?

Wrong.

The reason this clarification is necessary is because there are some recruiters who will send your résumé to companies without you even knowing! The problem with this is the company receiving your résumé does not know that you did not give consent, and then you can potentially look bad (without you even knowing), especially if a recruiter is over the line or aggressive with the company.

Don't let someone else tarnish your reputation with unprofessionalism. Guard your résumé closely and only give it out directly to companies or recruiters whom you trust and/or are comfortable with.

Speaking with Recruiters

Once recruiters have your résumé, you will most likely have a call with them so they can learn a little more about you and what you're looking to do next. This is very common and should be an easy conversation. The initial phone call should be casual but professional and fairly brief. You should not be surprised by any questions or made to feel uncomfortable in any way.

Be cognizant of how the conversation is going. A good recruiter will want to know your work history, where you are looking to go next in your career, how far you would be willing to commute, and possibly what your salary requirements would be.

Questions to Watch out for

Unfortunately, this is not always the case. All of the below questions (among others), including the many variations, are red flags. All of these questions are meant to work against you as negotiating leverage for a company; or are just plain nosy and rude.

Do not answer any of these and, if more than one comes up during a conversation, don't continue to engage with this particular recruiter. They are not worth your time.

Note: The same goes for company employees. They should <u>not</u> be asking you these types of questions either.

• What is your current salary?

• What is your salary history?

• What is the lowest salary that you'll accept?

• Do you have a family/kids?

• Do you own a home?

• How old are you?

• What year did you graduate college?

• Where are you from originally?

While some of these questions may come across as a recruiter innocently wanting to get to know you better, the fact is that <u>all</u> of these questions are offensive and none of his business.

If you reached out to a recruiter, then you will discuss what you are looking to do next as well as whether there are any current openings that might be a potential fit. And, if you are speaking to him about a specific role, then you will talk about your work history, your salary requirements, and also work to learn as much about the new role as he can tell you. That's it.

All of those other questions are totally irrelevant and, in some cases, illegal.

Recruiters are not your career counselor, friend, or mentor. They are **agents for a company** and are trying to earn a commission by placing you. Your relationship with a recruiter is also a *business relationship*. You don't need to answer offensive questions to be seriously considered for open positions, so don't allow them to make you feel small in any way. You are in total control of these interactions.

Finally, like with many of the topics in this book, use your gut. If recruiters (or anyone else you connect with) are making any types of disparaging or negative comments about you or your work history, you don't have to tolerate it. Your work history is what it is and you have nothing to apologize for. Don't get involved with someone who doesn't take the time to understand who you are and what you are looking to do next. Do not get drawn into a bad relationship. If it doesn't feel right, walk away and cut off all communication. There are plenty of good recruiters out there with whom you can work.

Knowledge Is Power

This book, especially this chapter, is meant to empower you on your journey to your next job. The more information you have about all of these moving parts, the more powerful you will be which will quickly translate into confidence.

Confidence impacts everything we do and everyone we meet in a positive way. Having confidence in yourself is the keystone to becoming a strong and successful job seeker, and this confidence will serve you best during the most important part of the process, the interview.

Chapter 8: The Negotiation

When this time of talking about salary and wages comes up, you will likely encounter some negotiation. Negotiation is something that many people are afraid of. People are afraid that if they ask for too much, they will offend the employer. People are also afraid that if they do not ask for enough, they will get offered lower than they would have if they would have just waited for the employer to offer first. Negotiating is still extremely important. Negotiation is the way that you can get what you want and the way that you can get what you deserve. It is the way to get the best possible salary and wage the company can offer you. Negotiation is a way to stand up for yourself and to show what you are truly worth it. In this chapter, we are going to look into negotiation and how to do it successfully.

Negotiating successfully

First, let's look into what you need to know about negotiation. Negotiation is not about arguing over wages; it's about knowing your worth. One of the things that you need to do to negotiate well is to know what you are worth before going into an interview.

Decide what you would want to make, and stick to it. You know that you are a great worker and that you are worth more than what some jobs are offering. You need to know the salary that you are comfortable with and the salary that you are looking for. If you do not, you will likely get a wage that you are not happy with. This may possibly be the cause of you not having the ability to be happy in your dream job. It can be the cause of stress in your life.

You may not always get what you negotiate for, but at least you know you tried. If you negotiate, you know that you are getting the best the company can offer you. If you do not negotiate, you may not be getting the best. This is because companies will usually offer you a lower amount of money that they are planning to pay first. The company will offer you a lower amount to see if you take it. This is not meant to be offensive toward you or to any other employees; it is just simply meant to save the company some money. The company likely knows they are starting out with the lowest possible wage, and they probably know the highest amount they can go to as well. For this, they usually expect there to be some type of negotiation involved in the hiring process.

Since companies are expecting a negotiation, it is not something that you need to be afraid of. When you negotiate, it actually shows companies you are confident and that you know your worth. Even though it causes companies to pay you more money and lowers their profit, many companies may actually be happy about the fact that you want to negotiate. It shows you can stand up for yourself, that you are serious about the position, and that you care about how you feel in the position as well. If you do not negotiate, the company may feel as though you are not as serious about the position as other applicants. For this, you might as well always at least try to negotiate salary during a job offer.

Another thing to think about when negotiating during a job offer is that you do not lose anything if they say no. It is not like they're going to lower their wage that they previously offered you. If you asked to make more money and you'll get it, great. Then your negotiations were worth it. If you ask for more money and you do not get it, okay. More than likely, the company will not be upset with you at all, and you will still be at the same wage you were before you asked. For this, it is easy to see that negotiation does not hurt you in any way. It can be uncomfortable at first, but maybe either leads to a better result or the same result, never worse.

When you are going to a job interview, you should know that negotiations could happen either during that interview or afterward during the job offer. You should never bring up wages during a job interview. If wages are brought up, they will be brought up by the person who is conducting the interview. If the person conducting the interview brings up wages, you can feel free to negotiate. This is because if the person who is conducting the interview starts talking about wages, it is likely that they are interested in hiring you. If you talk to them about negotiation during this time, it can save you from coming back for another trip if the salary is too low for what you need. If you ignore the chance to negotiate, you may not have a chance to negotiate later on.

Sometimes, wages are not brought up in interviews at all. If wages are not brought up in your interview, do not mention them on your own. If you get a job offer, they will be offered then. It is possible that the job is not interested in hiring you and why they're not talking about wages, or it could be that their policy is to wait to discuss wages until the job offer happens. Either way, you should wait until the company brings the wage issue up first.

If the wage is brought up during your job offer, then this is a completely appropriate time to negotiate. If you get a job offer, they will likely tell you how much you will make. You can decide if you want to take the job or leave it with this number. If you do not like the number they give you, you can negotiate it and see if they can give you more. Either you will end up making more money, or you will end up making the same amount you were going to make before you asked for the possibility of the salary to change. You will never make less money just from asking a question. For this, if we just brought up during a job offer, you might as well try to negotiate it.

As an example, you could say, " I am focusing on jobs in the variety of $70,000 per year". If you say this, the job will know exactly how much you were looking to make each year.

Again, it is important to have this number picked out before you go to the interview or before you get the call for the job offer. This is because you want to have the number ready in your mind before you have to say it. You want to think this number over to make sure that you are getting as much as possible while still being reasonable. For this, you probably want to choose the number when you have some time to think about it and not during an interview or job offer.

When you get this number in your head, stick to it. Do not lower it just because you want to take a position. Do not lower it just because you do not feel like negotiating. You know what you are worth and you need to stick to that. You should make what you feel you deserve. If you do not, you could resent your job later on with it.

When you are negotiating, remember to be confident. For this, if you are their top choice for the job opening, you will likely get more money than what they are offering. They could always go with someone who did not want to make as much money, but then they would be sacrificing the quality of the candidates that they were hiring. Most companies will not do this, so you do not need to worry about it.

When you tell the employer how much you want to make, they may offer you a lower amount. If they do this, consider negotiating. Try to meet in the middle. If the company can only offer you so much, there are other ways that you can get up to the salary that you want. To give an example, if you ask for $70,000 per year, but they can only offer you $65,000 per year due to their budget size, you could ask them for a $5,000 sign on bonus to reach your annual wage. You could tell them that this will get you up to the wage that you need for this year, and you will talk about next year when that time comes.

Another way that you can negotiate is their benefits. If a job can't pay you how much you want, consider asking them for extra vacation time. Most people are willing to work for less money if it means they can have more time off of work. As an example, if you took a $5,000 per year pay cut, you could get an extra week or two of vacation time to make up for it. This would give you more time to do things that you love to do, like to stay home with your family or travel. This extra time may possibly be worth the pay cut. If it is, consider negotiating with benefits if the job can't give you the wage that you were looking for. This may help you to feel better about making less money because you know you are still getting something out of it. It will also help you to know that the company is doing everything they can to give you what you need, even if they can't pay you the wage that you want to make.

When you are negotiating, things may not always go well. There may be times when you have to tell a job no when they offer you a number you cannot afford to take. If a job offers you a lower amount than you are willing to accept, and they're not in a position to negotiate with you, do not feel bad about turning them down. This not only means you need to fight for what you are worth, but it also means you need to walk away sometimes when a company is unwilling to give it to you. If you cannot negotiate a deal that you are happy with, consider moving on. If the company does not see what you are worth, they simply do not deserve you. This can be hard at first because you can see a company that seems like it would be your dream workplace, and then you find out that they cannot pay you as much as you want to make. However, another company will always come up sooner or later that sees your worth. A company will come up that actually deserves you. You just need to be patient and wait for it to happen.

When you are negotiating, remember to have a number in place before you go into the conversation. Otherwise, save this number for the job offer. You can discuss it and negotiate about it at that time. Also, remember it is okay to negotiate. They will not get mad at you for doing so, and you will not lose anything. You will either come out making more money or the same amount of money that you were before you talked about it. You will never make less money after negotiations. Remember when negotiating, you can likely meet in the middle. If the company cannot give you the amount you need, consider asking for a bonus or for additional benefits to make up for it. Also, remember that if your negotiations do not work, feel free to move on. You will find a company that knows your worth and that treats you the way you deserve.

Negotiation can feel scary, but it doesn't have to be.

Chapter 9: How to Handle Closing Questions

"If you were hired, what would you seek to accomplish in the first three months in the new job?"

Employers ask this question to gauge how you think about ramping up on your new role, how fast you are going to complete the onboarding process, and the types of standards and goals you have set for yourself, especially it being a new environment.

Remember that this time is also when you will be learning a lot about your responsibilities, your leaders, as well as the workplace etiquette. You will be adjusting and learning how to fit into the larger organization.

A part of your own interview preparation should be understanding what the particular job responsibilities and company structure will be like and to align it with your goals in order to ace this question.

Clearly, the longer it would take you to contribute significantly to the organization, the less admirable you would be. Therefore, avoid being vague or showing how you will probably still be adapting to the new environment. Employers today are interested in the fast-paced, innovative, and easily adaptable personnel.

A good answer would be, for instance, "Besides getting to know the team and fully tuning to the role, there is a lot more I'd like to accomplish in the first three months. In the first month, I want to learn the design of our marketing projects. After two months, I want to redesign and launch a project by tuning the efforts of the team, and after three months, I want to be able to track the growth of our marketing efforts."

"What questions haven't I asked you?"

Employers make this inquiry to assess your interest in the field and your enthusiasm and commitment to improving yourself as a worker in the industry. It offers a chance to showcase your ability to decipher information and establish anything you feel is important that they have not touched. Pointing out such a thing is what sets you apart and shows that you know what brought you here, how different you are, and your planned contributions.

Naturally, a person to be considered will be the one who seems truly invested in the industry and their personal development.

Be sure to emphasize your stage of career development, how you want to develop yourself professionally, and your long-term goals.

Avoid arrogance like showing you are the pinnacle of development with nothing extra to learn. Do not emphasize your idealized salary and fun job.

You could say, for instance, "My main focus is to continue developing my leadership and organizational skills, and I believe in constantly challenging myself to achieve more. My vision is around the big picture, and I want to exploit that ability the best possible way."

"What questions do you have for me?"

As the interview comes to a close, the interviewer is most likely to ask if you have any questions for them. It may feel as if you have covered everything in the course of your interview, but it is paramount to respond to this question rather than decline.

Your response should be guided by the knowledge of with whom you are interviewing. If it is your potential manager, then you can ask questions about the responsibilities of the position. If it is human resource personnel, however, you can ask questions generally about the organization.

You should prepare a list of various questions to ask during this phase in case some of them are addressed during the interview. Your response to this question will tell how keen you were during the conversation.

About the company you can ask:

- Can you talk a bit about the company culture?

- What are the goals of the company for the upcoming year?

About the role you can ask:

- Could you please share more about the daily routine responsibilities of the job?

- What is the major indicator of accomplishment in this job, from your perspective?

Avoid questions on topics such as off-work activities, interviewer's personal life, minor things you could answer yourself, as well as salary and benefits.

"Why should we hire you?"

By posing this question, employers are really asking to hear what you have to offer them and what other candidates may not. You should take this opportunity to reinstate your skills and prowess in doing some of the tasks you believe you can do best. Remember that the reason they need to hire someone is for them to solve a particular problem. Hence, your goal should be to show that you are the best person to solve their problem.

To prepare for this question, match your qualifications with the job requirements. Then, use anecdotes to illustrate your qualifications. Anyone can say that they have strong communication skills, but few can tell a story about how they have used those skills to negotiate a deal and successfully complete a major project.

Be sure to focus on your uniqueness to make yourself stand out among other applicants. Also, identify skills that may add extra value, including volunteer experiences that could have provided you with a unique outlook.

However, avoid bragging and assuming that you are the summit of progress. Present your response politely.

A typical answer would be:

"I feel that my experience in this industry and my ability to utilize a unique and work-related capability makes me a good match for this role."

Then explain how in a recent role you used this ability.

"When can you start working?"

This question also comes in the form of, "How much notice do you need to give to your current employer?" which especially applies to candidates who are currently working in another company.

This question can feel exciting and promising, but do not take it as the guarantee of a job offer. This question is not necessarily an indication that you will be offered this job.

The first thing to avoid is sounding desperate or like you are too eager, since this behavior may make employers suspicious of your motives for the job.

Even if they have selected you already but they do not tell you when they need you to start, some flexibility is allowed in determining a date that is good for you. If they give a date, inform them whether you are okay with it and avoid making a commitment you cannot keep.

If you are currently employed, the answer depends on the amount of notice that you need to give your current boss, or any other plans you may have. An appropriate answer would be, "My employer requires me to give one-month notice before I leave, so I would be able to start on [insert date]."

If you are not employed, you may want to begin working immediately to settle your bills. But do not underestimate the time you might need to gracefully tune yourself into the work mood. An appropriate answer would be, "I would greatly appreciate a few days, say a week or two, to clear the decks before I begin, but I can be flexible if you need me a little earlier."

"Would you work holidays and weekends?"

Simple as it looks, this question can effectively set aside individuals to be hired and those to be rejected. Some industries require workers to be flexible and be able to juggle work and other commitments because of frequent projects or long hours of operation needed at times.

Some tips when answering this question include being realistic about your time, but give your response a positive spin. For instance, you can say, "I have no problem working on weekends or holidays as long as I can schedule myself as early as possible."

Also, know your limits. Employers need confidence in a candidate who can keep time commitments. For instance, you can say, "Due to family commitments, I cannot commit to working every weekend and every holiday, but I can certainly give some of the days if need be."

You do not want to say a flat no and give your interviewer the impression that you cannot give up some of your free time for work purposes. Industries such as hospitality require this element.

Ideally, show some flexibility in your schedule, indicate that you have time management skills, and be confident and tactful. Avoid committing to a schedule that you cannot keep, and do not disclose more information about your schedule than necessary.

"How would you fire someone?"

This counter-intuitive question is raised especially when you are looking for a management position. The recruiter wants to assess if you have really got what it takes. Are you able to deliberate and fire an employee when necessary or just ignore the problem? Also, they are concerned that you will fire someone in a way that upholds the rights of the company and confidentiality of the employee when firing them.

Take this opportunity to demonstrate your management style and re-emphasize the leadership skills (such as emotional intelligence) you expressed in earlier parts of the interview. Show that you would never take firing someone lightly.

Avoid being mean when role-playing, as it is not the time to channel your perceived inner strength. Rather, respectfully show that you are firm and ready to make reasons for firing clear.

A reasonable way to fire is to say something like, "I'd first of all try to see if there is anything I can do to prevent having to fire the individual, such as constant communication and performance review. If it comes to the point that I have to terminate their contract, I'd engage with them privately without the knowledge of any other employee and explain the reason for termination."

Chapter 10: Bonus Questions

You really can never be too prepared in an interview. While you don't want to over-practice and make yourself nervous, it's still a good idea to keep up with potential questions and focus on thinking of all the loose ends that need to be tied up before the interview.

It's encouraged to come up with your own ideas of questions that the person conducting the interview would potentially ask. When you can put yourself in their shoes, you will be able to easily see the kinds of things that they might believe are the most important.

"How do you manage your stress levels?"

Stress is something that everyone feels. Even when we try our best to manage it, stress can still creep into our lives in seemingly small ways. The answer to this question is not about trying to deny that you get stressed. Instead, give a realistic method that you use in order to alleviate some of the symptoms. Here is a good answer:

"I make sure that I am managing my time first and foremost. When I can prepare and prevent it helps to keep the stress from creeping up in the first place. I do know my limits, however, so when I am feeling stressed I will do my best to take a break so I can come back with a clear mind, better ready to focus."

"How do you prioritize your tasks?"

We talked a lot about prioritization, and how you will need to do it first when you are organizing anything. But how exactly might you prioritize tasks? This helps the person conducting the interview to determine what's important to you and how you will gauge whether or not something needs your attention. Here's an example of what you might consider saying:

"I prioritize tasks first by how important they are. Then, I will number them and try to base what I'll do around this list. I also look to see if there are any tasks that I can quickly do to get out of the way. Sometimes it makes it easier to focus on the most important things if some of the smaller fluff is out of the way. I always ensure that I am focused on managing my time above all else."

"What steps do you take if someone you don't like in the office is really bothering you?"

We have all had that one coworker who seems to get really annoying. Maybe they chew their gum loudly every day, or perhaps they like to glance at your computer screen over your shoulder. Whatever it might be, you don't have to mention what they do that's annoying! What they will be looking for is how you might be able to handle this situation. Here's something you could say:

"I would first make sure that I am showing patience to them. It is easier to be annoyed with things on bad days, maybe if I were stressed about something outside of work. I would do my best to be patient and not let the little things bother or distract me. If I had a close relationship with them and felt comfortable, I might say something, like 'Would you mind not chewing your gum so loudly?' If not, then I would avoid the situation, and maybe wear headphones if permitted."

"What did you do to prepare for this interview?"

This is a good question that kind of breaks the awkward wall that was created surrounding this interaction. We don't always talk about how this can be a stressful time that we have to do our best to prepare for! This is a time when you will want to be honest above all else. Here's a good thing to say:

"I started my morning making sure I got enough rest before heading here so I could be relaxed. I got ready, got dressed in what I picked out this morning, and had a nice breakfast. The night before I made sure to go over my resume once more and freshen up on what questions I might be asked. On the way here, I listened to some relaxing music to reduce stress so that I would be able to relax and give honest answers throughout!"

"What are you hardest on yourself about?"

This is a good question to ask because it allows the person conducting the interview to get an idea of the kind of things you might personally struggle with. They will want to ensure that whatever you are saying is not something that will affect your job, but they also want to hear some personal honesty from you. Here's something that you might consider telling them:

"I feel as though I never do enough. Even when I have a fully productive day, I feel like there was more I could do. I think this is just because I understand how precious time can be and I want to make the most of my life, but that sometimes can cause me to be stressed and feel like I always need to be doing more!"

"What TV or movie character do you most relate to?"

This is a great question. It lets people understand first what it is that you enjoy. Which movies or shows do you like? What books do you read? After that, it can help them relate your personality to someone that they might know. When you answer this question, you will be able to give them a familiar idea of the type of personality that you might have. Here's an example, but make sure to pick something specific to you as well:

"I would have to say that I am like Ariel from The Little Mermaid. I am curious about learning more about the world, I enjoy swimming, and I have a diverse group of friends!"

"What is the last object that you fixed?"

This is a good question because it shows that you are a problem-solver. Even if you will never have to fix anything in the position that you are applying for, it still lets them know that you do have some handy skills and that you know how to get yourself out of certain situations. Answer this honestly, but here's an example of something you might wish to say:

"The last thing that I fixed was my garbage disposal. For about a week it wasn't working, and I was too afraid to stick my hand down in there in case that would be the moment it started working! Finally, I turned off the power and got a heavy-duty glove to help resolve the issue! My hand came out safe and the disposal is working better than ever!"

"When is the last time you lost something? Did you find it?"

This is a question to show your level of responsibility. It's easy to say that we hold onto all sorts of responsibility, but at the same time, practical questions like this actually help to show what your level of accountability is. Try and think of what the last thing you actually lost was and find a way to relate it to this job. Here's an answer that you might choose to say:

"The last thing that I lost were my house keys. I went to grab them and realized that they weren't in their usual spot. Then I retraced my steps and realized I had left them in the pocket of my pants which was in the dryer! They weren't lost for more than a few minutes, but I was able to remember everything I did so I could easily find them."

"Can you describe to me how you would make a PB and J sandwich?"

This question is not because the person conducting the interview is legitimately curious about how to make a PB and J sandwich. They might slip an easy question like this in there just to see what you thought process is. Where do you start? Are you going to begin by telling them to spread the peanut butter on the bread and then the jelly? Always start at the very beginning of the process and make sure you thoroughly explain all the steps so that they can really see what your thought pattern is. Here's a great way to answer this:

"First, I would start by gathering my ingredients, and making sure they're there in the first place. I'd place out a plate with two slices of bread, a knife for the peanut butter and then a spoon for the jelly. I'd consider who would be eating this as well. If it were me, I'd go heavy on the PB and light on the jelly. If it were for someone like my little sister, on the other hand, I'd cut the crusts off and make sure to put a scoop of extra jelly. I'd spread the ingredients on the bread and put the two pieces together. I'd serve the sandwich and then clean my utensils, putting my supplies away."

Chapter 11: Follow-Up

After your interview, send a thank you note to the interviewer. My recommendation here is that you send an actual thank you card (something plain) that you purchase at a local store. Ensure that your name and contact information is clearly printed on the inside of the card. If you have more than a few sentences to say, then it would be appropriate to send a personal letter instead of a card (or included with the card). For your thank you card to have any impact on your interview results, you need to send it immediately. If you wait a few days, the employer may have already made a decision before he/she receives your thank you card.

Your thank you card should be just that. Begin by noting how much you enjoyed meeting the interviewer and then thank him/her for considering you for the job.

If you decide to send a letter instead of a card, then you could add statements such as "I left with a better understanding of the role of … at your company." You might also say things like "I believe this position would be a good match for me (and you might state one or two of your best strengths that match the company's needs).

End your letter with a simple statement along the lines of "I look forward to hearing from you further."

If you have a letter of reference that you have not yet shared with the employer, you could insert it into your thank you letter.

It is also appropriate to send your thank you by email, although I would allow a few hours or even half a day to pass before you do this. Keep in mind though that emails tend to get deleted (almost immediately) whereas an actual hard copy thank you note tends to stay on the person's desk (often for a few days).

A question I am constantly asked by job seekers is "Should I call the employer if I haven't heard back within a few days?"

In response to this question, at the end of your interview you should have asked about the next step (and timelines) in the interview process. This information is one of your clues to deciding when to contact an employer after your interview. I would recommend you wait a few days after the deadline that the employer gave to you before calling. Some career experts would even say to wait a week, but I wouldn't go beyond this.

When you call the employer, you could begin the conversation by stating that you believed a decision related to the job was going to be made by such and such date. As this date has now passed, you were wondering if the timeline has been extended or whether a decision has been made.

If you are told that a decision has been made and you were not successful, be genuine in your thanks to the employer for considering you and taking the time to interview you. It would also be beneficial for you to end the conversation by stating your continued interest in working at the company if some other related job should become available.

There is one final note I should mention about what you should be doing after a job interview. Once the interview is over and you have sent your thank you card, then it is important to resume your job search. I have seen people sit around and do nothing for weeks after a job interview, only to find out they didn't get the job. Not only have they lost the job they were interviewed for, but they have potentially lost some other possible jobs that might have been available while they stopped their job search. Until you have received a definite job offer, persist in your job search.

The reality is that in some job interviews, you will be asked what you expect your salary to be. It is therefore important to research the salary range that could be expected for the position that you are applying for, along with a solid understanding of your own financial needs.

The following page provides some tips on salary negotiations.

SALARY NEGOTIATION TIPS

1. Don't bring up the topic of salary during your first interview unless it is mentioned by the interviewer.

2. Before a job interview, know how much money you need to make (what is your bottom line in order to meet your living expenses?).

3. Research the salary range for the job you are applying for. If you are asked what salary you are expecting, give an amount that falls within this range, or you could even state the range and say that you

would be willing to start at a salary that fell within this range. It could be to your benefit to appear to have some flexibility.

4. If you plan on stating a starting salary that is near the top of the range that you researched, then be prepared to explain why you are worth this salary.

5. When salary is being discussed, it is important for you to be aware of any benefits such as health insurance, pension, etc. It would also be useful to gain an understanding of opportunities to increase your base salary such as commissions, incentives, bonuses, or overtime.

6. It is important for you to clearly understand exactly what is expected of you in our job position before you settle on a salary amount.

7. Emphasize your value by talking about how you can help a company to be more profitable.

8. Avoid talking about your needs. It doesn't help to tell the employer about your car payments, or mortgage, student loans, or any other form of personal financial information.

9. Be open to options. Perhaps, there are some creative incentives for meeting specific objectives or goals that could increase your base salary.

Be realistic. If your training and previous job experience doesn't warrant that you should be placed in the top salary range, don't demand it. Whenever you are uncertain about a salary offer, ask for a day or two to think things over.

Chapter 12: Common Mistakes Made During An Interview

Having inappropriate or questionable content in social networking sites.

Remember, organizations do a background check before recruiting any one. About 70% managers in the recruiting department of different organizations have said that candidates make a grave mistake of uploading and posting compromising content in different social networking sites. Through the content, managers get to learn about writing skills and other insights of candidates.

Asking few questions.

This portrays that the concerning person is not interested in the job. The key is to ask not vital but smart questions. This way, you will not come across as a clueless or disinterested person.

Being overconfidence

This is mostly made by the younger generation. It is because they are conditioned and trained to have a strong sense of self-esteem, which most of the time, develops as overconfidence. They often make the interview process, only about them.

Turning Up Late

This should not happen in the first place which is why you don't need to take the chance. Set off very early. Its irritating how, only on the day of your interview that traffic and everything else seems to work against you. If it happens, you had better have such a reasonable excuse that it cannot be ignored. And at every opportunity, call in and let the interviewer know.

Fidgeting with Unnecessary Props

Please! Please! Please! Find a very diplomatic way of hiding your nerves and fears. Don't fidget with the pen, the books, folders, mobile phone, nails, your thigh or beard - don't do it. It sends too many wrong messages. For example, that you may be lying about something, or that you are not confident you can settle in the role, *etc.*

Unclear Answering and Rambling

If you don't know the answer to a question, say so and with a "sorry," but don't rant something totally off track. It isn't really the time to fool your way out. It can make the interviewer feel his/her intelligence is being insulted. And don't mumble. If the interviewer(s) has to ask what you just said more than three times, then you will start to lose it all on their score-sheet.

Speaking Negatively About Your Current Employer

If you don't have anything good to say about your former employer(s), please don't say anything. It won't go well for you if you do. The potential employer is likely to see himself in the same position when you finally leave their employment.

Discussing Money or Time Off

Unless it is put on the table by the interviewer, avoid as far as possible talking about salary packages, sick and holiday leave, or welfare policies. It soon becomes obvious you are not attending the interview for anything other than for money and people with that kind of dispensation hardly add any value to any role – they simply take!

Not Following Up

This is something not many candidates do after an interview – so the few that do it get an extra advantage. Even if you think your performance at the interview wasn't that great, you should still send the potential employer a short email message to say thank you for the opportunity and that you are still very enthusiastic about getting the job. Don't leave it days after the interview – do it the same day of the interview. The little extra effort only goes to show that you are a cut more serious about the role than all the others.

Assuming an Interview is an Interrogation

Too many interviewees assume that an interview is a process of the interviewer asking a series of questions and the interviewee finding responses to those questions. This is simply not the case. An interview is a two-way process. The employer is as much on trial in an interview as the interviewee. Be prepared to probe the interviewer for information and keep on with follow up questions until you are satisfied with your answers. Remember - this is your career that we're talking about! You don't want to wind up at a company who files for bankruptcy six months after you join, the signs of their impending doom having been painfully obvious to see had you just been a bit more assertive in your line of questioning.

Responding to a question without thinking

Sometimes in an interview we can lose focus. When this happens we either lose track of what we are saying or don't know how to respond to a question. The worst thing to do in this instance is to panic and blurt out the first thing that comes to mind. If you find yourself in this situation, choose a more constructive approach. Win yourself some time by repeating the question out loud to help you to refocus or ask the interviewer to repeat it. If you've forgotten what you are saying, admit as much to the interviewer and ask him/her to repeat the question. Never try to muddle through without having a focus on a question as it will only confuse you and the interviewer.

Not doing your pre-interview homework

Failing to make time to do your research on the employer, or planning how you can emphasize the qualities on your resume, or what questions you should ask the employer when prompted then you'll be doing yourself a huge injustice. The better prepared you are to answer questions about yourself, your career and your personality then the more likely you are to impress the interviewer and land that job.

Being Arrogant

Knowing within yourself that you have answers to all the questions being asked and being happy with it should not make you come across as arrogant. Don't start speaking or behaving like you've already got the job – you might be unpleasantly surprised. It will be far more profitable to your chances if you keep calm throughout the interview. If you know something that a panelist or interviewer doesn't know, control yourself. Don't let it show on the large screen of your ego. Nothing puts off a potential employer than an arrogant candidate – from the point it is first exhibited, most interviewers simply shut down from listening to you any further.

Turning the Weakness Question into A Positive

When interviewers ask about your weaknesses, they know we all have a few, so it's quite insulting of their intelligence if you try to paint yourself as someone without any. Instead, I suggest to think about a weakness that can be improved, but which does not impact on any of the core requirements of the job you are applying for.

Get caught lying.

A definite guarantee that you will not get the job is to lie during the job interview. If you are going to make a bold claim or state something that is not true, seriously think about your chances of getting away with it. Companies run background checks on potential hires. Whether it is about your credentials, accomplishments or your work history, honesty will usually be the best policy. It's tempting I know, but honestly what would it prove? If you lie about qualifications the employer will find out. If you lie about your career history the employer will find out. If you lie about your knowledge and experience you could end up getting into a very embarrassing situation in the interview itself!

Inappropriate humor.

Be confident, but avoid cracking jokes unnecessarily or saying things probably best left unsaid. A little touch of humor could work in your favor, provided that it is appropriate to the context of the interview. You do not need to be funny, especially when it is at the expense of appropriateness and formality. The last thing you want is for the hiring manager to think you are not serious about the job opportunity.

Getting personal.

A job interview is a formal meeting to assess if you are the right fit for a job. Everything in your personal life, your subjective opinions and how you are feeling should be left outside the door, and not be brought up during the interview.

Not appearing attentive.

It goes without saying that you should give 101% of your attention to the interviewer and respond to questions accordingly. Not smiling, playing with something on the table, bad posture, no eye contact, and fidgeting too much are behaviors indicating you are not paying attention. Additionally, checking your phone or answering calls are almost definitely job interview deal breakers.

Ask when the interview will end.

Nothing says "I don't care about this job and I am just wasting your time" like asking the interviewer how long the interview will be, or when will it end. You will also be doing just as much damage by constantly looking at your watch. When you are called in for a job interview, you are expected to make time for it, if you really want to get the job.

Bad-mouthing previous companies

It does not reflect well on you to talk negatively about companies on your resume. It's natural to have a few bad experiences, but be sure to paint them in the right light. If you talk negatively about a previous company, it implies that you will talk negatively about the company you're interviewing for now in the future. I've seen CEO's reject candidates at the last minute because of this.

Don't come under-dressed

This is a sensitive one. It's hard to know exactly what to wear. Overdressing typically means wearing a suit. Use your judgment, of course but always lean toward overdressing. 75% interviewers have said that most candidates turn up dressed shabbily or inappropriately for an interview. Follow the above attire checklist for creating a great impression.

Cursing

Please watch your language. Cursing implies that you don't communicate professionally in the workplace.

Conclusion

I believe the content of this book is very insightful. It has enlightened you on uncommon truths that are helpful in getting a job. Numerous people across the globe who have been unemployed for many years after graduating from tertiary institutions would have been enjoying better, happier and more prosperous lives as employees if they had access to the information in this book while they were fresh graduates. Numerous fresh graduates would unarguably get good jobs (even faster than they think) if they digest the content of this book and allow it to guide their job search activities.

You are very fortunate if you came across this book as a fresh graduate, as long as you will apply the principles it recommends in your job search activities. This book will save you years you would have wasted searching for jobs. It will also help you to make the best out of job opportunities you will come across, some of which you would have wasted. You are also very fortunate if you come across this book as a worker (and you are willing to be guided by its content) because it can help you get a better job, if you desire such. This book simplifies how to get a job. It enlightens the reader on what employers want from job seekers. It is a very reliable and authoritative manual for job seekers.

In competing for limited job opportunities, I am very confident that the job seeker who has undergone training in recruitment education has higher chances of getting a job than his competitors, even those who are more intelligent than he is, but lack recruitment education. The ideas that were exposed in this book have no place in the school curriculum (from the least to the highest level). As a matter of fact, I am very fanatical about the limitations of the educational system in its present form. The type of education that is offered to students in conventional schools does not adequately prepare them for real life challenges (after graduation).

This is one of the reasons most graduates have difficulties meeting real life challenges after numerous years of leaving school. This is why I recommend Supplementary Education to every graduate. Ideally, supplementary education ought to have a place in the school curriculum to assist students to be more focused and productive when school days are over. Most unfortunately, it does not. This shows that much of what students are taught in school are things they do not need to succeed in real life. By this token, most of what students need to survive in the real life are not taught in the school. I once argued that

"An uncommon truth among most graduates is that most of what they need to know in order to achieve a bright future are things that are not taught in school. This, however, is not a way of discrediting the value of education. The society cannot do without school. The school system produces professionals the society cannot do without. Your years in school should not be considered a waste of time and resources. The point being made is that what you learnt in school is inadequate for your success. The deficiencies of the school system make room for Supplementary Education. Supplementary Education is complementary, auxiliary and ancillary education. You will have no meaningful success in the future, even as a graduate, if you lack this type of education, no matter your course of study, your grade or the school you attended."

As noted above, it is impossible to have any meaningful success in the real life (i.e. life after school) in the absence of supplementary education. The major factor that underlies the failure of most graduates in real life is the absence of supplementary education. This highlights the necessity of this type of education. As seen above, one of the reasons many graduates remain unemployed after years of leaving school, despite being exceptionally intelligent, is that they lack Recruitment Education. They are ignorant of what employers want from job seekers. They are ignorant of what they need to know in order to be able to convince prospective employers that they are the best candidates for the positions they applied for.

This book in your hand is aimed at providing you with one of the supplementary education you need. This is, perhaps, the first type of supplementary education you need to succeed in the real life. It is called Recruitment Education. It is an education that prepares you for getting a job, if not for getting your dream job. This is the aspect of life's challenges it is geared towards addressing. There are other types supplementary education which are geared towards addressing the challenges in other areas/aspects of life. Since success is essentially concerned with striving for balance in all areas of life, this supplementary education is inevitable for everyone, even non graduates, who sincerely and conscientiously desires to achieve a meaningful and successful life.

www.ingramcontent.com/pod-product-compliance
Lightning Source LLC
Chambersburg PA
CBHW070345220526
45467CB00001B/249